DARE TO LAUGH

Devotions for Those Full of Years

Elizabeth H. Van Liere

SonRise Devotionals
Lighthouse Publishing of the Carolinas

DARE TO LAUGH – DEVOTIONS FOR THOSE FULL OF YEARS
BY ELIZABETH H. VAN LIERE
Published by SonRise Devotionals
an imprint of Lighthouse Publishing of the Carolinas
2333 Barton Oaks Dr., Raleigh, NC, 27614

ISBN: 978-1-941103-81-4
Copyright © 2015 by Elizabeth H. Van Liere
Cover design by Goran Tomic
Interior design by AtriTeX Technologies P Ltd

Available in print from your local bookstore, online, or from the publisher at:
www.lighthousepublishingofthecarolinas.com

For more information on this book and the author contact: betty.vanliere@gmail.com

All rights reserved. Non-commercial interests may reproduce portions of this book without the express written permission of Lighthouse Publishing of the Carolinas, provided the text does not exceed 500 words. When reproducing text from this book, include the following credit line: *"Dare to Laugh – Devotions for Those Full of Years* published by Lighthouse Publishing of the Carolinas. Used by permission."

Commercial interests: No part of this publication may be reproduced in any form, stored in a retrieval system, or transmitted in any form by any means—electronic, photocopy, recording, or otherwise—without prior written permission of the publisher, except as provided by the United States of America copyright law.

Scripture quotations taken from the HOLY BIBLE NEW INTERNATIONAL VERSION r. NIVr Copyright © 1973, 1978, 1984 by International Bible Society. Used by permission of Zondervan Publishing House. All rights reserved.

Scripture quotations taken from the New King James Version®. Copyright © 1982 by Thomas Nelson, Inc. Used by permission. All rights reserved.

Scripture quotations taken from THE MESSAGE. Copyright © by Eugene H. Peterson 1993, 1994, 1995, 1996, 2000, 2001, 2002. Used by permission of NavPress Publishing Group.

Scripture quotations taken from the Amplified® Bible, Copyright © 1954, 1958, 1962, 1964, 1965, 1987 by The Lockman Foundation (www.Lockman.org). Used by permission.

Scripture quotations taken from the New American Standard Bible®, Copyright © 1960, 1962, 1963, 1968, 1971, 1972, 1973, 1975, 1977, 1995 by The Lockman Foundation (www.Lockman.org). Used by permission.

Brought to you by the creative team at LighthousePublishingoftheCarolinas.com: Cindy Sproles and Brian Cross.

Library of Congress Cataloging-in-Publication Data
Van Liere, Elizabeth.
Dare to Laugh – Devotions for Those Full of Years / Elizabeth H. Van Liere,
1st ed.

Printed in the United States of America

Praises for *Dare to Laugh*

Elizabeth Van Liere's new book, *Dare to Laugh*, is a joy to read. Her writing style reads easily. Each segment of her book wraps up with a short prayer, scripture and thought provoking question that all tie in nicely with each one. Particularly poignant segments, at least for me, are the ones concerning her husband's battle with cancer, as well as handling her grandson's accident that resulted in him needing ongoing special care. Although her book is geared toward senior adults, it can certainly be enjoyable for younger readers as well.

~ Cathy Roberts Montrose Christian Church Seniors Ministry Team

In Elizabeth Van Liere's second book, *Dare to Laugh*, we find a treasury of thoughtful meditations on being joyful through thick and thin places. A book about joy might have been superficial, or, so unilaterally positive as to be useless in the daily grind, but, not so this book. Elizabeth takes an honest look at life as it is,

and, dares us to believe joy is still possible. As a reader, you know that you are looking into the heart of a seasoned traveler – one who has walked arm in arm with Jesus for many years – and has ben listening as he spoke. As a Licensed Professional Counselor with a specialty in Christian Counseling, I will enthusiastically recommend *Dare to Laugh* to my senior clients.
~ *Dr. Steve Warner*

In *Dare to Laugh: Devotions for Those Full of Years,* Elizabeth Van Liere invites readers to laugh and hone in on God's plan and purposes during the inevitable struggles of old age. This book is honest, poignant, and fun - filled with hope and the promise of a beautiful eternity to come.
~*Jeanne Dennis Author and Host of Heritage of Truth TV*

Thank you, Betty Van Liere, for your wise words, encouraging words, and beautifully crafted words. *Dare to Laugh in the Face of Lemons – Devotions for Those Full of Years* is a book to be savored and treasured.
~ *Marlene Bagnull author and speaker Director of Colorado & Greater Philly Christian Writers Conferences*

Table of Contents

Introduction ix

Eternity 1
Laugh in the Face of Death – I Dare you 2
God's Gift 13
Walk in the Hope of the Lord 19
Shine Brightly, Precious Light 25
Home 31
The Echoes of One Moment 37
A Cry from the Heart 43
Two Sides of Life 49

Being Groomed 55
What's So Funny? 56
Jesus Joy 61
Beware! 67
Speak Up 73
To Do or Not To Do 79
Don't Be Foolish 85
One-Track Mind 91

Perseverance 95
Soft Answers 99
The Greatest Wonder 105
Out of the Mouths of Babes............................. 109
I Love You, Jesus.. 115
To Be Like Jesus 121
More Blessed to Give 125
From Bad to Worse to Better to Best.............. 131
I Paid for It, I'm Gonna Eat It 137

Wisdom, Grace and Wrinkles 143
Aging? For or Against? 144
Whose Glove is This?.. 149
Do I Hafta Do It?... 155
Surprise! 161
Be Happy... 167
Sometimes You May Say No............................ 173
Mirrors 179
Loneliness 183
Now, When It's All Said and Done 187

Dedication

To the One who fills my life with laughter.

Job 8:21

Introduction

Laughter is one of God's gifts to us. Where does it go when someone we love dies, we lose a needed job, illness disrupts our lives or a child takes a wrong turn?

Even when our personal life is running on track, we cannot escape the dark clouds. News items in the morning paper or on the evening news cause us to wonder if joy has disappeared from the world.

Is it wrong, then, to grieve? The Bible tells us David lamented, Elijah mourned and Jesus wept. . . permission to cry, granted.

It has been said happiness comes from the outside while joy comes from within. What can bring that joy back into our lives? When should laughter overcome our tears?

It is my hope, by seeing God at work, these devotions will return lost laughter to you.

Lessons I have learned, and am still learning, have prompted this book. My thanks go to those who have helped it come alive.

Gail Marvel and Leslie Jones, thank you both for taking time to critique the devotions. Eddie Jones and Cindy Sproles, partners at Christian Devotions, I thank you for starting me on this path and walking with me on it. A special thanks to my family and friends because without their encouragement this book would not have seen these pages.

May this book bring glory to God and bring joy to you, my readers, because God's love will shine brighter for you.

ETERNITY

Dare to Laugh in the Face of Death

Laugh in the Face of Death— I Dare You

Someone has said, "The day we are born is the day we begin dying." For a long time, this attitude cast a cloud over my life. It made me wonder—did we arrive on this earth to see an end before we began?

As a child I played with dolls, fell asleep on the floor with my head on our dog's stomach, argued with my siblings, learned to roller skate, cried because I hurt myself when I fell. I ate what my mother put before me and went to bed on time. I had fun.

I didn't need to be spanked. A frown from my dad broke my heart and my disobedient will.

But when a dear aunt died, I learned sorrow and how to cry in a different way—because my heart, not my arm or my head, hurt. One by one a grandfather, a grandmother, another aunt, and an uncle left this world for what I had been told was heaven. Fine, wherever that was, but I had grown to love them and their death meant more crying.

After World War I, my mother received word her parents had died in the Netherlands during the war. She locked herself in her bedroom. I listened as she sobbed. I had only met them once, so I barely knew them. Yet I sat in the living room on the couch, wrapped my arms around myself, rocking back and forth. I cried with her and for her. Hours later, when she came out of her room to make dinner, I gently patted her arm and received a teary, upside-down smile in return.

It hurts even now to remember. Did it mean laughter had gone forever? For a while, it seemed so, until I found someone with a loving touch. Someone who said, *"I am the way, the truth and the life. Come unto me."* His name is Jesus.

Years have passed. My parents have died. My husband, too. There are more and more empty spaces, as friends go on this mysterious journey without me. With each departure, a lonely ache fills my heart. I've learned through the sadness there is happiness. It took time after the loss of a loved one, but I'd find myself chuckling at memories . . . joyful moments with those who'd passed. I saw death was not such a bad thing, rather as a step into eternal happiness. That's when I dared to laugh in the face of death.

Even as my own body ages and slows, I find a great peace in laughing. It's in those times of deepest pain the comfort of Christ shines through and we remember a fondness of the one we loved . . . the we miss. There you have it. A smile in the midst of heartache.

Through the years, church, Bible study and friends opened my heart, and this wondrous place called heaven became real to me. I met the One who died for me. He forgave my sins, so death will not be an ending. It will be another beginning. When someone I love dies, of course, tears fall. But I dare to laugh through those tears because I know I will join those I love. I will be with them. I will meet Jesus and, wonder of wonders, live with Him forever.

After that, we who are still alive and are left will be caught up together with them in the clouds to meet the Lord in the air and so we will be with the Lord forever.

1 Thessalonians 4:17 (NIV)

Eternity

"What are you afraid of?" the pastor asked as he began his weekly sermon.

The thought sprang to my mind: eternity. I'm not afraid of death. I'm afraid of eternity.

It scares me. The "foreverness" gets me. No beginning. No ending. Here on earth I am secure, in-between a beginning and an ending. I wake up in the morning when the sun brightens the day and go to bed at night when darkness steals the light.

Someday, time will vanish and eternity will begin. When that happens, we'll go on forever. Facing the unknown makes shivers creep up my back. What will life be like? Will it still be called life? Will I know those I have loved on earth – my husband and children, parents and friends?

Since kindness will fill everyone's hearts in heaven, my flat notes should be ignored when we sing praise songs. Maybe I won't have to sing. Perhaps I can praise Him with devotional thoughts from my heart like Kahlil Gibran, the poet, hoped to do. He expected to meet his unpainted paintings and unwritten words in heaven.

I will tuck the thought away for now. Seeing Jesus will surely inspire greater words than I have been able to formulate here.

Jesus has been my guide all these years, touching pain with healing, turning heartaches into joy and transforming dark skepticism into bright belief.

I have no need to fear eternity when someday I will wake renewed and see God's glory before me. Until then, let me wait with joy for my entrance into His presence, anticipating marvels I can't imagine. When it happens, I'll throw off the wrappings of time and see Jesus.

All my questions will be resolved, and I will be glad to exchange today for the forever of what God has in store for those who believe in Him.

Prayer

Eternal God and Father, why should I be concerned about what is to come? Laughter will pour from everyone's mouth. Tears replaced with smiles. Sadness forgotten. I can hardly believe it, but I know—Yes, I know—it is true. Thank You for filling my heart with this wonder, God. I can hardly wait. In Jesus' name, Amen.

A Step Further

He will wipe every tear from their eyes. There will be no more death or mourning or crying or pain, for the old order of things has passed away.
Revelation 21:4 (NJV)

Moving On

Step by step, I'll walk into the future, laughing and unafraid.

Question

Are you ready to welcome eternity?

Because of the Lord's great love we are not consumed, for His compassions never fail.

Lamentations 3:22 (NIV)

God's Gift

David, my fifteen-year-old grandson, sat in his wheelchair and stared at Joni Eareckson Tada's program on television. I watched for signs of emotion on his face, but there were none.

Did he realize Joni, too, was handicapped? Did her message of hope mean anything to him—this boy with the blank stare? I wiped away a tear.

David was nine when he was struck by a car. After a month of prayers by family and friends, he woke from a coma, no longer able to speak or move. Every morning my son lifted him from his bed, settled him in a wheelchair, and later, carried him back to bed. Four times a day his parents mixed up his food and fed him through a tube in his stomach. Whenever I visited, I never knew if David was looking at me because his eyes seemed to look in different directions. The real David never reappeared.

When Joni's inspirational presentation ended, my son switched to a comedy video.

"I really don't feel like laughing," I said. "Not with David just sitting there. Everything the comedian says sounds silly. This is so stupid."

A loud huff interrupted my outburst. I turned to David, afraid something was wrong. Short bursts of laughter came from him whenever the comedian said something funny.

I grabbed David and hugged him. Our David might be locked in his broken body, but God had given me a gift of hope. He showed me, through David's laughter, David was with us after all.

Last July, we celebrated David's thirty-eighth birthday. With the use of a Hoyer lift, his parents now move him to and fro from his hospital bed to a wheelchair. He is still fed through the tube in his stomach and is still unable to speak.

I fly to Virginia for a yearly visit. When I walk to his bedside, I am rewarded with a smile. When I prepare to leave for home again, I get the same empty stare. Even that is a bonus, for it means he is aware. *Am I imagining it or is there a tear in his eye?*

My tears mixed with laughter when David responded to a video. "David, I can hardly wait for the day when we are in heaven, and I see you leaping and jumping and running once again." David smiled a crooked smile. I smiled too. I could finally see beyond today into tomorrow.

Prayer

Heavenly Father, wipe away my tears that I may always see beyond sorrow. Fill my heart with laughter as I remember your constant love and compassion. In the name of Jesus, Amen.

A Step Further

The LORD himself goes before you and will be with you; he will never leave you nor forsake you. Do not be afraid; do not be discouraged.
Deuteronomy 31:8 (NIV)

Moving On

God's love surrounds us, even when we don't realize it.

Question

Does God's love give me hope and make me laugh?

… but those who hope in the Lord will renew their strength. They will soar on wings like eagles; they will run and not be weary, they will walk and not grow faint.

Isaiah 40:31 (NIV)

Walk in the Hope of the Lord

"I walk like an old lady," my seventy-five-year-old friend grumbled.

"Tell me about it," I said. "I walk like one, too." (I hate to admit it, but I have joined the *senior* citizen group.) One of these days, when wisdom overrules pride, I may decide to use a cane.

At birth, I began my hike up the mountain called life. Momma and Papa held me up and led me step by step until I shook off their helpful hands. "I can do it myself," I said and took those first few steps alone as they cheered me on.

Through the years, my steps became more self-assured. At one time, I told myself the path to the left looked more exciting than the boring one I was on. Off I went, only to find myself in a dark forest, stumbling over boulders and brushing briars out of my way. Exciting? It didn't take long before I turned back to what had seemed so boring.

Years later, I see the summit ahead. I find myself inching forward on unsteady feet instead of hiking with a long steady stride. Now, I keep my eyes focused on the path in front of me. Reality has met me face to face, and I've learned to say thank you when someone offers an arm to keep me from falling. I can't deny it. I *am* an old woman

No matter. I am grateful for all these years, especially since I learned someone has climbed beside me all this time. He is the One who pulled me back and said, "Go *this* way," when I turned down a wrong fork in the path. He helped me over the rough spots I encountered. He showed me views I didn't know existed. When I began this climb, I thought I would hike this mountain alone, but all this time God has walked beside me.

Our walk may slow us down, but one day we'll soar like eagles. We'll run and not grow weary. Most of all, we'll walk and not be afraid of falling. It makes me laugh, just to think of it.

Prayer

Heavenly Father, we believe your promises are true. Help us look forward to the day when we will walk and not grow faint. Bless our family and friends who watch out for us. In Jesus' name I pray, Amen.

A Step Further

For all the promises of God find their yes in him. That is why we utter the Amen through him, to the glory of God.
II Corinthians 1:20 (RSV)

Moving On

The best way to walk well is to walk with the Bible.

Question

What do the promises in Isaiah 40:31 mean for me?

Then shall the righteous shine forth as the sun in the kingdom of their Father. Who has ears to hear, let him hear.

Matthew 13:43 (KJV)

Shine Brightly, Precious Light

Another light has gone out in our world, but it shines brighter than ever in heaven. A friend has finished her race.

Her daughter, Jeannie, called to tell me. "Last week Mother told me she couldn't wait to sit at the feet of Jesus. Yesterday she said, 'It won't be long now. Today or tomorrow.'" Jeannie paused. "She died last night."

A tear slid down my cheek. I wiped it away. There was no need to cry. I could picture Irene sitting at her Savior's feet.

Irene was one of those comfortable people. Comfortable to talk with. Comfortable to be quiet with. Comfortable to laugh with. Sometimes we cried together. She shared her love of her Lord in an easy way, never realizing how much she was letting her light shine. It told me not only was she comfortable with me, she was comfortable with her Lord.

Was she perfect? No. Occasionally bitterness and unkindness took hold of her, and she would spout off to me about the person at fault. Her bright light would flicker but flame brightly again.

"Oh, dear. I shouldn't have said that. It's not what Jesus wants me to do. Please forgive me." Her apology was as much to Jesus as to me.

When a person lights a candle, they can hold it to another's unlit candle. As the flame touches the cold wick, the unlit candle begins to burn.

By her life, Irene's candle must have started a flame burning in many other candles. I am one of them.

Prayer

Lord Jesus, you are the Light of the world. Thank you for this light which shone so brightly in Irene. Help me, I pray, to pass this light on to others. Amen.

A Step Further

For God, who said, "Let light shine out of darkness," made his light shine in our hearts to give us the light of the knowledge of God's glory displayed in the face of Christ.
II Corinthians 4:6 (NIV)

Moving On

Light the candle God gave you,
share the glow.

Question

Does my candle shine as brightly as
that of my friend?

For this world is not our home; we are looking forward to our city in heaven, which is yet to come.

Hebrews 13:14 (NLT)

Home

A notice arrived at my church from an assisted living home: *Wanted. Someone to play hymns for our clients.*

"Why not?" I said, and a friend seconded the idea. Neither of us plays the piano but my boom box and a variety of our CDs bring remembered joy to the ladies. My friend and I now fill a half hour each week playing familiar hymns for them.

Six to ten ladies, all residents of the home, come to listen weekly. They are as varied as a garden of autumn flowers, fading away as they spend their days being cared for by strangers.

Some of the ladies sing-along while others just listen. "This is my favorite," one dear lady says each time we play *What a Friend We Have in Jesus*.

"Do you recognize the singer?" Puzzled frowns appeared, but when I reminded them, "Tennessee Ernie Ford," smiles quickly replaced frowns. Tennessee Ernie Ford was familiar.

Darlene made her regular remark as she straightened herself in her chair, "I can't sing. I had a stroke."

"Sing in your heart," I said. "God will hear you." Later I saw her lips move as she sang silently.

Margaret is deaf and stares into space, alone in a soundless world. I hand out a song sheet and she reads the words, perhaps living in memory.

You never know the mood Anne will bring with her. One morning she was more upset than usual. An aide had moved her walker.

Before the music started. I tried to soothe her. "I'll get your walker back when you are ready to leave," I promised.

Despite my words, the scowl on Anne's forehead deepened. Once again she grumbled, "She shouldn't just take it out of my hands."

Sweet Mary maneuvered her wheelchair with hands twisted by arthritis. Her ninety-two-year-old smile and her *thank you* when I was ready to leave, warmed my heart all the way home.

Each week, someone asks, "Who are you?" "What are we doing today?"

One speaks only Spanish. With a fierce look on her face, she shoots her hands up and waves them like a conductor, urging the silent audience to participate. She may not know English, but music speaks in any language.

Once these women had husbands, raised their children, and had homes. Most of them, now widows, are in failing health. From a house with several rooms, filled with belongings and memories, their lives have shrunk to one room with a closet and a bathroom. Just the basics moved with them. Cars, household items, souvenirs that held meaning, were sorted through, sold, and discarded by their children. Only memories traveled with them.

Perhaps their best memories are the hymns, remembered from childhood, treasures stored in their hearts. These cannot be taken.

These ladies are in God's waiting room. Soon those who are believers in Jesus will leave this small shelter and move into a mansion, a place with many rooms. This is the promise Jesus gave.

They are not alone because you and I are in God's Waiting Room. As Christians, we look forward to the fulfillment of His promise.

Prayer

Heavenly Father, along with these displaced women who are looking forward to their heavenly home, I, too, anticipate the move with joy. Your promise lights the way ahead. Amen.

A Step Further

For we know that if the earthly tent we live in is destroyed, we have a building from God, an eternal house in heaven, not built by human hands.
II Corinthians 5:1 (NIV)

Moving On

One day we'll call heaven home.

Question

Some people say, "I want to go to heaven. But not today." If the Lord calls me today, am I ready to step out of God's Waiting Room into the joy of heaven?

I will praise God's name in song and glorify Him with thanksgiving.

Psalm 69:30 (NIV)

The Echoes of One Moment

Several years ago, I was privileged to travel to Israel. I visited places Jesus walked, and the Bible opened before me. As I walked where Jesus had walked, I felt His presence beside me.

On the hill above the Sea of Galilee, I stood where the crowd stood when Jesus taught the Beatitudes. *Were the people struck by the same touch of wonder that fell on me?*

Our guide led our group to another hill. Here the shepherds saw the angels and heard of the birth of our Savior. My heart pounded at the thought of the glory falling on them.

Each place touched my soul, but I took home the awe and reverence I found in a small church. . .the little church at the well. Here it is said Mary met the angel of the Lord. When we entered the darkened church, all talking ceased. After a moment, one person began to sing, *How Great Thou Art*. Soon the rest of us joined. Some of our voices wavered, while others sang true. The song became our worship and rose to the domed ceiling. It was like a promise of singing yet to come.

Tears streamed down our faces as we ended with, *In Moments Like These*. I wiped my tears and the song folded into memory. All eighty singers walked silently from the church and stood blinking in the sunlight. The presence of the Lord had been with us in that place.

We do not need to go to Israel to feel God's presence. Sing to Him with others or alone. Read His word. Find quiet moments to speak with Him. You'll find God is just a prayer away.

Prayer

Heavenly Father, help me open my heart to Your presence no matter where I am worshipping. Fill me with awe and reverence for You. In Jesus' name, Amen.

A Step Further

Therefore, since we are receiving a kingdom that cannot be shaken, let us be thankful, and so worship God acceptably with reverence and awe. . .
Hebrews 12:28 (NIV)

Moving On

God gives us special moments to hold in our hearts.

Question

What moment has filled my heart with God's joy?

*Why am I discouraged? Why so sad?
I will put my hope in God!
I will praise Him again—my
Savior and my God!*

(Psalm 42:11 NLT)

A Cry from the Heart

Christmas carols poured from my car radio. Since there was no one to hear my raspy voice, I sang along. Christmas changes when your children and grandchildren move away, but the season brings memories back to life. What fun, giving the children special gifts while reminding them of the meaning of Christmas: the birth of the greatest gift of all—Jesus.

Such good times. Those boys! They hunted until they found the presents I thought I had hidden. Years later, they told me how they opened the gifts and carefully rewrapped them. Oh, I must look for those pictures of my daughter's first Christmas doll. How lovingly she held it. Now she cuddles her grandchild.

A voice on the car radio interrupted my thoughts and the Christmas songs. The announcer cleared his voice a couple of times. He choked on his words. "Twenty elementary school children and seven adults have been shot and killed in their school rooms by a young man on a rampage of hatred."

How could this happen? My heart raced. I pulled into a vacant parking space and cried for those parents whose children would not open their carefully chosen gifts. My heart broke for the families of the adults who were murdered. *What will their Christmas be like this year and years to come? There will be no sweet memories for them.*

I watched the television as the other parents, the fortunate ones, hugged their children . . . kissed them, comforted them, and hurried them home. Never once did they let their eyes meet those whose children had died.

"Where were You, God, when this happened?"

In my heart, I heard the answer. "I was there when my Son died, and I was there when these died."

Mike Huckabee said, "God *was* there during the killings. He was in those teachers who protected the children. He was in the police who stormed the school, not knowing if they were to be met by a barrage of bullets. He was there in the hugs and tears of others who shared in the losses of friends and relatives."

When sorrow overwhelms us or darkness overshadows us, we dare to hope. Let us believe God is there to love us, comfort us, and to remind us of His promise, "I will never leave you nor forsake you."

Prayer

Heavenly Father, I dare to hope because I believe You are God. I want to be one of those who shares Your love, who hugs the grieving person, and who tells others You are there beside them. Amen.

A Step Further

Why am I discouraged? Why so sad?
I will put my hope in God!
I will praise Him again—my Savior and my God!
(Psalm 42:5 NLT)

Moving On

Faith leads into hope, and
the answer to every, "Why, Lord?"
I can laugh because I have hope.

Question

Where do you find peace?

Laughter can conceal a heavy heart; when the laughter ends, the grief remains.

Proverbs 14:13 (NLT)

Two Sides of Life

The doctor hesitated and cleared his throat. "Mr. Van Liere, the MRI points to multiple myeloma."

"Myeloma. That's cancer." I grabbed Chet's hand.

"Cancer?" my husband said. "Can't be. Must be a mistake." He pulled his hand away from mine and slapped the desk.

"I'm sorry, Mr. Van Liere. There's no mistake. It's the reason you've suffered such severe back pains this year." The doctor's voice was quiet, but the words thundered in the room.

"What do we do now?" Chet asked.

"Chemo." The doctor's smile encouraged us. Hope often comes with a smile and you go on toward the light.

In an instant that light faded. We entered a scary world filled with hour-long injections of poison to kill the cancer cells. Blood counts. Chet's continuing pain. Did I feel resentful as our golden retirement years melted into cloudy days? How could I when Chet remained cheerful—especially at the clinic.

Each time we came, he asked the solemn nurses the same question. "Are you bats ready for my blood again?" Each time they obliged him by breaking into laughter.

In our apartment he held onto the wall, bit his lip against the pain and stumbled to bed to lie down. No need for him to be cheerful then, but neither did he become grouchy or ornery.

Did I cry in front of him? No way. Only during his fitful naps did I allow my silent tears to fall. *Keep praying. Keep smiling. Keep joking.* Afraid, perhaps, to face the uncertain future, I adopted these mottos.

But, oh—the last time I took him to see his doctor, Chet, without objection, let me drive. He let *me* drive. I blinked back tears as the strong, tough man I married disappeared.

"Your blood count is too far off. You need to enter the hospital." The doctor wrote instructions for his nurse to admit Chet.

Three weeks later, at 4 a.m. the hospital called. Chet had developed pneumonia. I drove the dark streets, begging God, "Please help him."

Chet lay in a coma, silent, still. I sat beside his bed and rubbed his hand—yearning, praying, hoping—to warm up his cold fingers. "God," I whispered, "I know You're here. But it's so hard."

Three days later, Chet left for his heavenly home. He left without saying good-bye.

It was no longer necessary to hide my tears as one dreary day after another shuffled past, dragging me into despair.

Then God whispered no to the darkness. "Choose," He seemed to say. "Fall or fight." A writing class at Glen Eyrie, Colorado, became available. I signed up and chose to turn the page in my life.

The Glen Eyrie countryside invited me to stop, listen to my heart, feel God's presence, sense His touch in the rose gardens. I realized God's eternity in the red cliffs surrounding the park.

The writing workshops renewed my spirit. The instructor fed us writing tips and soul-filled scripture. My heart overflowed with God's peace, and for the first time in months, although grief lived in my heart, I could laugh again.

God does this. He gives us tears to ease our sorrow and laughter to bring healing. Have you been laid low by sorrow? I dare you to trust God to raise you. His timing is perfect.

Prayer

Thank you, God, for the tears that bring release and the laughter that lightens the heart. Amen.

Moving On

Yes, the Lord has done amazing things for us!
What joy!
Psalm 126:3 (NLT)

Question

Which is more important to God,
my tears or my laughter?
Whether we cry or laugh,
God's heart is touched.

BEING GROOMED

Dare to Laugh in the
Face of Life's Lessons

What's So Funny?

Did Jesus ever laugh? Let my pastor tell you. He has the ability to make you look past a few verses of Scripture and see the whole picture. For instance, when Mary approached Jesus at the wedding in Cana and said, "Their wine is gone." Jesus replied, "Dear woman, why do you involve me? My time has not yet come."

We nod our heads and go on to read the rest of the story. Stop a moment. Free your imagination. Watch as Jesus put His arm around His mother. He turned His face to the side and hid His smile as He replied to her, "It's not my time yet, Mother." He shook His head and laughter escaped as He proceeded to do as she asked. Love brings laughter.

I believe Jesus laughed. Can't you see Him with children on His knee, laughing with them, free from the divisiveness of the Pharisees? He said He and His Father, God, were one. God had/has a sense of humor. Didn't He invent long-legged, long-necked giraffes? And how about humans? What an assortment He created—all shapes and sizes, in many colors, each group with their own language and all with mouths that sometimes open before their brains say, "Hold it!"

I should know. I often speak before thinking. When this happens, a cloud *of how stupid can you get* rolls over me. Red-faced, I apologize, then remind myself of my husband's favorite words. "Oh, well. A hundred years from now nobody will know the difference."

But I know the difference because God grooms me through the life lessons of age and experience. Oh sure, I've done some pretty ridiculous things, pulled some pretty spiffy stunts...things I was sure seemed good at the time but really weren't. I can stand back and laugh now but at the time—well, it wasn't so funny.

If I let life keep me in a tizzy, I'd never find happiness and so, my husband's wisdom keeps me from taking myself too seriously. I can be overly self-conscious at times. Especially when I look in the mirror. Like the time blood suddenly gushed from my nose as I ended a short talk at a women's retreat. "Oops," I said. "I have a bloody nose," (as if the ladies couldn't tell).

I grabbed a tissue and raced toward the restroom. Two friends followed, doused paper towels with cold water and wiped the blood from my blouse while I held another three or four tissues to the bloody fountain.

With my bodyguards—one in front and one in back of me—I returned to the auditorium and slipped into a seat. Embarrassed? A bit, until I told myself, "No big deal. At least you finished your speech."

There are times when laughter covers a pain. Proverbs 14:13 says it all: "Even in laughter the heart may ache, and joy may end in grief." (NIV) And so it is. We see a loved one off at the airport or train depot and we laugh and wave good-bye. Left alone, tears of loneliness begin to fall. In the same way, when a loved one has passed from our sight, we smile and laugh through our tears because we know they've merely gone ahead. We will see them again in heaven.

So, what's so funny? It's this strange joy God gives us through good times and bad, a foretaste of the time when there will be no bad times. Instead, all will be joy and laughter. He grooms us to be fully His.

But now I come to You and these things I speak in the world that they may have My joy made full in themselves.

John 17:13 (NASB)

Jesus Joy

It happened a zillion years ago, on a sunny day. Five friends and I took our umbrellas, opened them and held them over our heads as we walked a busy street in Chicago. Like a troop of solemn soldiers, we marched straight ahead, single file. No talking. No laughing. At every street corner we stopped, swung our umbrellas to the side, and as a group, stared upward. We bit our lips to stay sober as people passed by and stared.

Someone smirked. Another person giggled. The dam burst and our laughter poured like a flood onto the street. The five of us broke into hysterical laughter. We doubled over, held our stomachs and gasped with our silly, ill-gotten mirth.

Perhaps we, like some of today's youth, those with tattoos, purple and orange spiked hair and numerous body piercings, were stating, "Hey. Look at us. We're special, whether you know it or not."

The fun of the moment made our day. I blush to think how stupid we were. Yes, stupid, because I've found another kind of happiness as I've grown older and wiser. It's called Jesus Joy.

These days I don't have to act silly, color my hair in shocking colors or wear a diamond in my tongue to attract attention. I already have Jesus' full attention. He knows me and tells me I am special. He loves me and He loves you too. What better joy can we find?

The "fun" we had when we were young cannot compare to the full measure of joy we receive when we take the presence of Jesus into our lives. I'm so glad I said, "Yes, Jesus. I believe you. I want to be part of your family. I want Jesus Joy in my life."

Want a full measure of joy instead of a half-full cup of fun?

Prayer
Giver of everything good, I thank you for filling my life with everlasting joy instead of good-for-the-moment fun. I accept it with a grateful heart for it is given by your Son, Jesus. Amen.

A Step Further
"... and though you have not seen Him, you love Him, and though you do not see Him now, but believe in Him, you greatly rejoice with joy inexpressible and full of glory."
I Peter 1:8 (NASB)

Moving On
Jesus Joy will brighten even the darkest days.

Question
Jesus already knows me. Do I know Him well enough to experience His joy?

Watch and pray that you may not enter into temptation; the spirit indeed is willing, but the body is weak.

Matthew 26:41 (RSV)

Beware!

The back roads will get'cha every time. Take the day I took a shortcut. A quarter of a mile down the side road, I glanced at the speedometer: Forty-five miles per hour. *Oops. Slow down. This is a thirty-five mile zone.*

I eased my foot off the gas pedal, but my car was built with a special magnet that attracts black and white cars with flashing blue lights. A police car shot out of a parking lot and rolled in behind me. The lights flashed. *Oh, no.* I pulled the car to the edge of the road. The police car followed and seconds later the uniformed officer tapped on my window. *Yuck.*

"Ma'am, you were driving too fast. This is a thirty-five mile zone."

"I know, but I had slowed down." For good measure I added, "Before I saw you."

He shrugged his shoulders. "Sorry, Ma'am. You were speeding. I have to give you a ticket."

I questioned if a few tears would help, but with his bulldog face I had my answer before the question actually dropped from my lips. You'd have thought he would have taken pity on my gray hair and wrinkled face. I sighed and surrendered my license, proof of car ownership and insurance papers.

The policeman checked my information and flashed me a sweet smile. He gave me his card. I smiled back just as sweetly.

When I got home, I gave my best martyr's look and told my grandson about the event.

"Gran'ma," he said in his best parental voice. I could already tell there was no sympathy. Not from him. "I thought you knew better."

"Well, I'll remind you of this when you get your first ticket." I smiled and hung my traffic ticket on the refrigerator.

At the same time, a thought assailed me—what's with this heavy foot? Does older mean faster or am I trying to show I'm still gung ho? There are reasons for the road signs. I could have hit a child. Killed a man on a bike. I shuddered at the thought. Of course, my grandson was right, I should know better.

Alas, it's not just driving that gets me into trouble. When temptations dance before my eyes, I swerve off course and do what I know I shouldn't do. Afterwards, guilt slaps me on the shoulder and I wipe away tears of regret. I have no excuse for going the wrong way because I know what God desires.

Just as my grandson said, "I thought you knew better." Just as signs along the road warn us when to stop, slow down or turn, God gives us His directions in His book for a holy life.

Why do something we know isn't right? Let's turn back onto His way when we've taken the wrong route. Better yet, choose the right way before proceeding.

Disregard His directions? Disobey? We should know better.

Prayer

Father, you have shown me the right way, the best way. Forgive me for taking a shortcut for it only leads to disobedience. In the name of the One who never turned away from your will, Amen.

A Step Further

For the eyes of the Lord are on the righteous and his ears are attentive to their prayer, but the face of the Lord is against those who do evil.
I Peter 3:12 (NIV)

Moving On

If we break the law, sooner or later punishment will follow.

Question

Does knowing that I disobeyed (sinned) cause my tears to flow?

Jesus said to them, "If you were blind, you would have no sin; but since you say, 'We see,' your sin remains."

John 9:41 (NASB)

Speak Up

On a plane en route to Phoenix from Cabo San Lucas, a stewardess passed out U. S. custom forms. "One per family," she said.

A young woman seated next to me raised her hand and pointed at her companion. "We each need one."

The stewardess laughed. "Oh, oh. We found a couple living in sin."

"Living in sin and loving it," the woman's partner said in a loud, cocky voice.

A second stewardess piped up. "If it's okay for you, then it's all right."

Words burned on my tongue. *No. You're wrong. God instituted marriage, not just living together.* I bit my lip, the fire died, and I said nothing.

What if I had quoted the Bible to the stewardesses or the couple, or those around me, and told them what God says? I shrank into my seat. Undoubtedly, they would have laughed behind their hands and called me a crazy old lady who should mind her own business.

Once I *had* dared to make it my business. One of my granddaughters shared a house with her boyfriend. I called her on it.

"Oh, Gran'ma," she said. "Times have changed."

My reply made her roll her eyes. *"If times have changed it's because people have changed. God said, 'I, the Lord, do not change.'"* Malachi 3:6 (NIV)

God doesn't change, but I, like a coward, *silently* asked God to touch the hearts of the couple and the stewardesses. I turned chicken and reverted to my old self.

When we say yes to God it should be as true a commitment as the marriage vows. In my head, I hear Jesus. "Crazy old lady. Why didn't you mind God's business?"

Prayer

Father, forgive me for the times I sit in silence. Help me share the joy of knowing You. Amen.

A Step Further

Then I said, "Ah, Lord God! behold, I cannot speak: for I am a child." But the Lord said unto me, "Say not, I am a child: for thou shalt go to all that I shall send thee, and whatsoever I command thee thou shalt speak."
Jeremiah 1:6, 7 (KJV)

Moving On

Let the Holy Spirit have the last word.

Question

Do I let silence muffle my conscience or do I let the Holy Spirit open my mouth?

*I do not understand what I do.
For what I want to do I do not do,
but what I hate I do.*

Romans 7:15 (NIV)

To Do or Not To Do

Our two dogs, Uber and Bear, were in the house alone for two hours. It must have been exciting to find the bathroom door open. I'm convinced they took turns hauling the trash out of the wastebasket. Uber, our Blue Heeler, probably got into the trash first, while Bear, the miniature Aussie, followed close behind. Their lips are sealed. They'll never tell who instigated the deed.

"It took me ten minutes to clean up the trail of chewed up, shredded tissue from the bathroom to the kitchen," my grandson grumbled. He was the lucky one to arrive home first. "I chased those nasty creatures outside with the broom."

As my grandson vented about the two troublemakers, I choked back my giggle. "We need to remember to keep the bathroom door closed," I said.

"And the lid on the kitchen waste basket," David added.

Funny? Yes, but only to me, who didn't clean up the mess. Insignificant problems like these are easily forgotten. After all, they're just dogs and the open door and tempting wastebasket called them to come and enjoy.

But when it happened again, I didn't laugh. That morning, I walked from my room into the hall. Trash strewn from the other bedroom trailed Bear. The culprit still had tissue in his jaws.

"Aha. You're the one." I rested my hands on my hips and scolded him. "Naughty Bear. You're bad."

Bear gazed at me and pulled his best adorable, "I'm sorry" act, curling his body around my foot. The naughty dog routine seemed to break his heart.

I relented and patted him. "Okay, I forgive you." It was enough. He jumped up and tried to lick my hand.

Later it struck me I, too, had spread trash. It concerned something I couldn't wait to tell a friend. Gossip.

Like a star on a sitcom, I rushed to share the news. "Carla said she saw Jason eating lunch with his wife's best friend."

My friend raised a brow. "Oh, no. Poor Marcia. You know, I always wondered about him. Do you suppose we should tell her?"

I shrugged my shoulders. "I'd rather not be the one to tell her. Let's wait." The two of us spent another fifteen minutes discussing the incident. We even snickered about it.

Three days later, an invitation from Jason and Marcia's best friend arrived. They had planned a surprise birthday party for Marcia.

Guilt pounded at my heart. Why had I repeated such a damaging story before I knew the truth? I'd even enjoyed the telling.

God didn't pat me on the head when I regretted spreading trash. Instead, my conscience accused me. *You're just like everyone else. You did it again.* I chewed my lip. Why doesn't someone rescue us from these horrid habits?

The Apostle Paul says for us to ask and God will do it—through Jesus Christ the Lord!

I had to ask forgiveness before the guilt went away and I learned a valuable lesson. Now every time I'm tempted to gossip, I remember this experience and quickly veer away. Now I choose "to do" what God asks me to do.

Prayer

Father, it is You who shows us how wrong we are. It is You who forgives us when we repent. It is You who takes us on a better way, the way of Jesus. Thank You, Father, thank You. Amen.

A Step Further

So I advise you to live according to your new life in the Holy Spirit. Then you won't be doing what your sinful nature craves.
Galatians 5:16, 17 (NLT)

Moving On

Take the trash bags to the dump.

Question

Do I want to serve the law of sin or the law of God? (**Romans 7:25**)

O God, you know how foolish I am; my sins cannot be hidden from you.

Psalm 69:5 (NLT)

Don't Be Foolish

King Solomon should have included this in his proverbs: *If you do something foolish never tell your kids what you have done.* I should have typed those words on a card to carry with me. Which foolishness was worse, what I did or when I told my daughter? It was one of those days when a hundred necessary *to do* items occupied my mind. Topping the list—keep my appointment for a haircut at my friend's home.

Slow down, I thought as I drove a tad over the speed limit. *Slow down.* I repeated as I tore out of my car and rushed into my friend's home.

"Same as usual?" Jean asked.

I nodded, and the process of beautifying me proceeded. *How can a haircut take so long?* I wiggled in the chair, thinking of all I had to do.

"Sit still, or I'll chop too much off," Jean said.

I sat back, closed my eyes and tried to relax.

Chunks of hair lay on the floor. The plastic cape was removed. "Looks great," I said. "Thanks. Lots to do," I tossed her a smile and scurried out the door.

Outside, a rumble greeted me as I approached my car. My heart sank when I realized I hadn't turned the motor off. A bright side? Maybe. I was in such a rush I'd gotten out of my car and failed to turn it off.

This is where Solomon's wisdom would have come in handy. I could have kept this a secret, but no. One foolish deed led to another. I told my daughter. I felt myself shrink a bit as I received the look only a daughter can give. It was one of those, *Oh, Mother,* looks. I'll be hearing about this for years to come.

Why hadn't I kept quiet? Even as the too-late thought ran through my mind, it occurred to me there is someone who always knows everything I do, from doing my best, or being foolish, or committing sin. This someone is God. Letting the car run may just make Him smile and shake His head. The sins I commit are another matter.

Stop before you do something you'll regret. Look before you plunge ahead. Listen when God says, "No."

And remember, God sees our sins, so it's best to confess and repent, or better still, stop sinning.

Prayer

Father in heaven, I know you see when I've done wrong, but even so, I want to acknowledge my sins. I want to confess them because only then can I be forgiven. Amen.

A Step Further

Nothing in all creation is hidden from God's sight. Everything is uncovered and laid bare before the eyes of him to whom we must give account.
Hebrews 4:13 (NIV)

Moving On

Sin doesn't like our walk with God.

Question

Does knowing God sees me make it easier for me to keep from sinning?

Then we will no longer be infants, tossed back and forth by the waves, and blown here and there by every wind of teaching and by the cunning and craftiness of men in their deceitful scheming.

Ephesians 4:14 (NIV)

One-Track Mind

Do you have a one-track mind? I don't. My mind jumps from one thing to another, never finishing the first project before going on to the next. Too often I've rubbed my head and admitted I goofed again.

For instance, I put six eggs in a pan of water, intending to make deviled eggs. I set the pan on the stove and turned the dial to high. *I'll turn this down in about five minutes.* I and headed to my computer room to work.

Twenty minutes later a loud popping interrupted my concentration. "My eggs!"

The water in the pan had boiled away. Black smoke swirled from the stove along with a nasty odor. Two of the eggs had burst their shells and my dogs were enjoying the grayed leftovers that had hit the floor.

"Stupid me," I groaned. "When will I learn to do one thing at a time?"

My mind may have a habit of jumping the track, but not when it comes to Paul's words in Ephesians: *Don't get distracted by someone preaching the opposite of what we have been taught. Set your mind on Jesus and His teachings. Don't let other doctrines sway you from the truth.* I completely understand it.

Why? Other doctrines are like eggs that boil too long. They are hardened and fit only to be thrown out. They do not proclaim Jesus as the Son of God. They do not tell you to believe He died and rose again so your sins are forgiven.

As Paul urges, stay on one track. The right track—the Bible.

Prayer

Heavenly Father. Help us to believe your truth. Jesus is that truth. Keep us steady, unwavering and holding on to all we have learned, that the way to You is through Jesus and Jesus alone. In His precious name. Amen.

A Step Further

Jesus answered, "I am the way and the truth and the life. No one comes to the Father except through me.
John 14:6 (NIV)

Moving On

Do not swerve from the left to the right.

Question

In John 6:68, Jesus asked his disciples if they wanted to leave Him. Would my answer be the same as Peter's?

. . . we also rejoice in our sufferings . . .
Romans 5:3 (NIV)

Perseverance

Suffering has many faces; each one is different. Just ask my grandson.

Two years ago Sam and his wife, Melodie, felt led to plant a church in an unchurched area. Today they are still waiting for an affordable home to rent in that city.

"Is this really what God wants us to do?" Sam asked. "Is this the city where He wants us to start a church?"

Helpful friends and relatives offered opinions. *Find an internship in a large church. Look for a less expensive area. Don't you think you should get a full-time job?* Each suggestion only frustrated Sam more.

"I can't go backwards," he said.

Even Paul's words in Romans struck a blow: Rejoice in suffering. Wait on the Lord for His timing. More of Paul's words gave them a clue. God works in us during hurtful periods. *Our suffering produces perseverance; perseverance, character; and character, hope. And hope does not put us to shame, because God's love has been poured out into our hearts through the Holy Spirit, who has been given to us.* Romans 5:3-5 (NIV)

I continue to pray for God's answer as Sam and Melodie continue to mature in God's grace. This I believe—God's answer will come when the time is right.

Live with hope, wait with patience, do not quit. This is the clue to perseverance.

Prayer

God, rejoicing in our suffering is not easy. We need Your help to do this. We want to rejoice because the end result is not a "maybe" hope, but a realization that the answer is in Your hands. Thank you, God. Amen.

A Step Further

Now faith is being sure of what we hope for and certain of what we do not see.
Hebrews 11:1 (NIV)

Moving On
God's answer is worth waiting for.

Question
Can I rejoice, even when I'm hurting, because I know I am in God's hands?

A soft answer turns away wrath, but a harsh word stirs up anger.

Proverbs 15:1 (RSV)

Soft Answers

"Get ready to do some fishing, boys," I said to my two grandsons. "Put your poles in the trunk, get in the car and buckle up."

An hour later my friend, Mae, welcomed us to her home beside the Gunnison River.

"You're right on time," she said. "The hot dogs are ready to be eaten." Two hungry boys did a magic act with the lunch, and soon Mae and I visited while the boys tried to catch those fish.

As anglers in canoes and rubber rafts drifted past, the boys began to whisper.

On the drive home I asked, "What were you two talking about this afternoon?"

Luke scowled. "Gran'ma, our Sunday school teacher said something that wasn't true."

Oh, oh, teacher. You stuck your foot in it, I thought. "Maybe you misunderstood, Luke. What did she say?"

Before he could answer, David spoke up. "She said a soft answer turns away rafts. But it doesn't work."

Luke finished the story. "We spoke real soft, but the rafts didn't turn away."

I choked back laughter and explained. "Boys, she told the truth. She said *wrath*, and that means anger. You can't make a raft that floats in the water turn aside by using a soft voice, but you can stop someone from being angry by not getting angry yourself."

"I told you she wasn't lying," Luke said as he punched David's side.

"No hitting each other, boys," I said. "If you fight I might forget to use a soft voice."

Later, a chance came for me to put this bit of wisdom into practice. A friend called and asked me to go to lunch with her. "This is a bad time, Marsha. I need to defrost the freezer. Next week would be better."

I began to put the frozen foods into an ice chest, and a friend from another city called. "Hi, Betty. I'm passing through town. How about meeting me for a quick lunch?"

I closed the ice chest and hurried to meet Gloria.

Marsha called that evening. "You couldn't go to lunch today? I saw you go into Denny's with someone else when I drove by." Before I could answer she said, "Don't worry. I won't ask you again."

Her words were the match that lit my fire. "No big deal," I said. "If that's how you feel, so be it."

I slammed down the phone. *Huh. Who cares?* But wait. What about my grandsons' observations about soft answers and rafts. Not rafts. Wrath—anger. With a few words, I had tossed years of confidences and giggles – our friendship – into the wind.

I called my friend back. "Don't hang up, Marsha," I said. "Let me apologize. Gloria was passing through town and asked me to go to lunch. She left right afterwards. I meant to call you and explain, but I started defrosting the freezer and I forgot. I'm sorry."

After a moment Marsha's weepy voice said, "Thanks for calling, Betty. I hated being angry at you. Please forgive me."

Our friendship bloomed. Another lesson learned. Soft answers to another person's anger does turn away wrath. They quench *our* anger, remove the other person's and we do what God desires of us—live in peace and joy with each other.

Prayer

Lord Jesus, help me put aside another person's anger by answering them in love. Teach me to be gentle. I ask this in Your precious name. Amen.

A Step Further

Everyone should be quick to listen, slow to speak and slow to become angry, because human anger does not produce the righteousness that God desires.
James 1:19-20 (NIV)

Moving On

Anger and pride walk hand in hand.

Question

Do I let the angry words of others rule my life?

I praise You because I am fearfully and wonderfully made; Your works are wonderful, I know that full well.

Psalm 139:14 (NIV)

The Greatest Wonder

A drab, colorless day met me this morning. "Great," I muttered. "Just what I need. A yucky day."

I shuffled to the bathroom. Ate cold cereal. Didn't bother making coffee. Half-heartedly read a devotion, more out of habit than talking to God.

Yuck. Shuck off this dark mood. Go outside. Look around. It's time for the hummingbirds to return.

Sure enough, two of them dived at the feeder I had filled the day before.

Sunshine entered my day, carried on the wings of God's little wonders. "Thank you, God," I said.

One bird chased the other one away, like a bossy child saying, "Wait your turn. I was here first."

"Silly birds, there's plenty for both of you," I whispered. Maybe they heard me, for each found a place on opposite sides of the feeder. Their green wings drummed the air while they drank the gift I put out for them.

My dark mood disappeared. When you look at God's world you see His wonders and guess what? One of them is you. Even greater is this: He loves me and He loves you.

Prayer

Father God, You graciously share Your world of wonders with me. I thank You for them all, but most of all, joy fills my heart, because You love me. In the name of Jesus. Amen.

A Step Further

Great are the works of the Lord; they are pondered by all who delight in them.
Psalm 111:2 (NIV)

Moving On

God's gifts fill my life with sunshine.

Question

How can I show my thanks to God for loving me?

From the lips of children and infants You have ordained praise ...

Psalm 8:2 (NIV)

Out of the Mouths of Babes

Rain poured on the first day of a family weekend vacation. My four great-granddaughters had looked forward to paddle boating, swimming and at least two outdoor picnics. Instead, they were stuck in an apartment, bored and restless.

Six-year-old Julia frowned as she looked out the window. She put her wishes into words. "I sure would like to go swimming."

I hugged her. "I'm sorry, honey. Maybe the sun will shine tomorrow."

Julia chewed her lip. "I know. But it's really God's decision."

God's decision? Where did this child obtain such wisdom and acceptance?

A moment later the spell was broken. "Want to play checkers?" Julia asked.

"Only if you let me win."

"No way, Gran'ma." Julia's grin told me I had better watch out.

Checkerboard loaded with chips, the battle began. Even as we played another battle raged in my brain. Just last week a mechanic had pulled a nail out of one of my tires.

"Ma'am," he said. "Look at the tread on these tires. It's worn too far down. You need new tires. These are dangerous."

"But I have plans to visit my sister in Florida. I can't afford to do both."

He held his hands up in surrender. "It's your decision."

I stared at the checkerboard. The mechanic said, "It's *your* decision." But perhaps Julia's words, "It's God's decision," were a nudge from God.

"Gran'ma!" Julia's impatient shout startled me.

"Oops. Sorry, Julia." My hand moved a red checker. Isaiah said God would answer before we called. Had He led me to someone whose knowledge could keep me from an accident?

A disgruntled voice again broke into my thoughts. "Gran'ma, it's your turn."

"Sorry, honey. You made me think of something important. Good thing you woke me up."

Julia giggled. "I woke you up? If you're asleep, I'm sure gonna beat you."

We finished the game, which Julia won. "Not fair," I grabbed her and tickled her. I'd won, too, for I took the mechanic's warning to heart. God had spoken through him before a tragedy occurred. I put my Florida trip on hold and bought new tires.

If you listen when a child speaks, you may smile at their sweet childlike way. Or you may hear God speaking to you through them and you will say, "All right, God. I hear You and I'll do what You say."

Prayer

Father, You have promised to guide us, but we don't always want to listen. You show us how unwise we are, simply by way of a child's words. Amen.

A Step Further

Trust in the Lord with all your heart and lean not on your own understanding.
Proverbs 3:5 (NIV)

Moving On

God cares, even in the smallest matters.

Question

How much me and how much God?

"As the Father has loved me, so have I loved you. Now remain in my love..."

John 15:9 (NIV)

I Love You, Jesus

Twenty years ago my daughter's marriage broke up. Soon after she and her four young sons moved in with us, my husband died. The children booted much of the sadness out the door and replaced it with laughter, but their energy also brought days when I longed for peace and quiet.

An envious friend said, "You are so lucky to have grandchildren nearby. I love spoiling mine and playing with them when they come on vacation."

"Easy for you to say," I told her. "Spoil them? Play with them? I'm back to the days when my children were young. I love the boys, but I'm the boss when my daughter is at work. I cannot spoil them. I'm too busy. 'Why do I hafta' clip the grass after I mow?' 'There's nothing to do!' 'Gran'ma. You don't understand.'"

As the days rolled on, "Mother Knows Best" (substituting Gran'ma for Mother) and "Because I say so," found their way back into my vocabulary.

Bloody battles were fought, the kind boys love—I had to break them up. Often I shrugged my weary shoulders and said, "Just wait 'til your mother comes home. I'll let her deal with you."

Except for a question now and then, homework always brought some of those desired moments of peace and quiet. One day Luke, the eleven-year-old spoke up. "Gran'ma."

"Yes, Luke?"

"I love you, Gran'ma."

Had Luke said what I thought he said? Without being prompted?

"Wow, Luke. You made my day." I walked to where he sat figuring his math problems and hugged him. "I love you, too, honey."

"Aw, Gran'ma," he said and ducked down under my arm.

A bell rang in my heart. Luke's "I love you, Gran'ma," made the moment sparkle, a precious gift to warm my heart.

I hummed as I began preparing dinner until suddenly, some of my words echoed back to me: *God, why is my world so torn up? It would be nice to fly to a beach in Florida and lie in the sun. But, God. You don't understand.*

I was just like the boys. Worse—when was the last time I said, "I love You, God. I love you, Jesus."

God's love fills our lives. Let's tell Him, "God, I love you."

Prayer

Heavenly Father, I love You. Jesus, my Savior, I love You. Holy Spirit, thank you for bringing my love to heaven, Amen.

A Step Further
The name Jesus means love.

Moving On
Love is an action verb. Use it.

Question
How do *you* feel when someone says I love you?

So Jesus explained, "I tell you the truth, the Son can do nothing by himself. He does only what he sees the Father doing. Whatever the Father does, the Son also does."

John 5:19 (NLT)

To Be Like Jesus

My five-year-old grandson's dad had been absent from his life for two years, yet David said, "This is how my dad takes off his shirt."

He crossed his arms in front of his stocky chest, grabbed the left side of his tee shirt in his right hand and the right side in his left hand, and peeled his shirt off. He flexed his make-believe muscles and said, "I wanna be like Dad."

David only remembered what he had seen his father do. To be like his dad, he had to spend time with him.

Jesus is someone who lived so close to His Father that He mirrored Him. When Jesus began His mission on earth, He chose twelve men, disciples, to walk with Him. They saw how He stayed in contact with His Father through prayer. They saw in Jesus a life filled with love and service for others. Step by step, they became like Him.

Jesus is no longer on earth with us, but we, like the twelve men He chose, can become His disciples as well. If Jesus is the One you want to resemble, walk with Him through the gospels, learn from Him, and pray to Him. His love will change you.

Prayer

God, Jesus poured love to everyone He met. Help me, please, to be like Him. In His precious name, Amen.

A Step Further

Dear friends, we are already God's children, but he has not yet shown us what we will be like when Christ appears. But we do know that we will be like him, for we will see him as he really is.
I John 3:1-2 (NLT)

Moving On

To be like Jesus is to live in love.

Question

Do I cast a shadow of love?

...You'll not likely go wrong here if you keep remembering that our Master said, "You're far happier giving than getting."

Acts 20:35b (The Message)

More Blessed to Give

At four years of age, my granddaughter, Jennifer, lived in the "my or mine" stage of life. She had been visiting her grandfather and me, but the time had come to return home. She watched as I packed three small gifts in her suitcase.

"This is for your mommy, this one is for your daddy, and this one is for your best friend," I said.

"Gran'ma, isn't there anything for me?"

"Honey, we bought you several things while you were here. Don't you think it'll be fun to surprise Mommy and Daddy and Tessa?"

Tears filled her eyes. Her lower lip quivered. "But Gran'ma, I think it would be fun to s'prise me, too."

I wiped away her tears with a tissue and kissed her cheek. "Maybe there will be a surprise when you get home," I said. I held back a giggle as I pictured her when she found the pretty necklace I had hidden in the suitcase. A surprise for her.

The years rolled by since that day. Now my family sees to it I have all I need or want. Surprise gifts come now and then and I'll admit, I love it. I was living in a "my or mine" stage. I forgot we are blessed so we can bless others.

Hurricane Sandy's flooding in the fall of 2012 opened my heart. I watched a sixty-year-old woman on TV cry to a reporter,

"Home. I want to go home." She pointed at the rubble where her house once stood and cried out, "But there is no home."

I looked around at my home, saw all I had, and my heart broke for her. This lady needed a surprise gift. My gift could not replace all she had lost, but others gave as well and the one small gift grew. That's love in action.

We give surprise gifts to our grandchildren because we love them. There is a world out there that needs our love as well. Let the world see someone cares.

Prayer
Heavenly Father. You hear the hurting cries of people everywhere. I have so much. Help me share and let my giving bring hope to those in need. Amen.

A Step Further
You have been treated generously, so live generously.
Matthew 10:8b (The Message)

Moving On
My heart hears the cries. Let me open my hands.

Question
Do I need Open Hands surgery?

And you will hear of wars and threats of wars, but don't panic. Yes, these things must take place, but the end won't follow immediately. Nation will go to war against nation, and kingdom against kingdom. There will be famines and earthquakes in many parts of the world.

Matthew 24:6a-7 (NLT)

From Bad to Worse to Better to Best

For several months, one of the north/south roads in our town was closed by construction work. Huge machines chopped up the road and the broken concrete chunks gave way to red dirt and rubble.

The next time I drove to town, I found the east/west main thoroughfare had suffered the same fate. An orange helmeted worker held up a sign, SLOW. As if I could do anything else.

I glared at the man and muttered, "I hate this. I will be so glad when this is finished." I chewed my lip as I waited in line for traffic to move.

Day after day the work poked along, one scoopful of dirt at a time. Then came the day I drove to town and saw the cones were gone. "Yippee!" I shouted. I didn't care who might hear me. Even the bumps in the road had vanished. Traffic moved as though I drove on velvet. Stop lights once again ordered me to stop or go. My smile met smiles from passing drivers and my frustrations faded away.

An old saying popped into my head. Things must get worse before they get better—just like the street.

The Bible agrees. I read the newspapers and watch the news on TV, and life looks like a snowball that is growing larger and larger as it rolls toward a huge catastrophe.

Sadness. Worldwide earthquakes. Tsunamis, wildfires, ocean storms—a flick of the TV dial shatters my illusion of man's complete control of everything, even the universe. The insurance companies call these disasters acts of God. *Hmmm.*

There are other disasters. Sex trafficking of young girls and boys happens daily. Guns take innocent lives at our schools and streets while bombs destroy villages in faraway countries. Our moral freedoms are being chipped away, law by law.

The world struggles with evil, this kind caused by man. Despair fills my heart. Where can I find hope? God promises an end to this in Matthew 24:13-14. So if we endure, if we cling to hope in God, we will see how He will heal and bring joy back into the world.

Prayer

Heavenly Father, You alone can give Your broken world the hope it longs for. You alone can bring back laughter. I pray for this in Jesus' name, Amen.

A Step Further

Then I saw thrones, and seated on them were those to whom judgment was committed. Also I saw the souls of those who had been beheaded for their testimony to Jesus and for the word of God, and who had not worshiped the beast or its image and had not received its mark on their foreheads or their hands. They came to life, and reigned with Christ a thousand years.
Revelation 20:4 (RSV)

Moving On

Laughter is revived by hope.

Question

Why have I hidden my hope from others?

*Like a city whose walls are broken through
is a person who lacks self-control.*

Proverbs 25:28 (NIV)

I Paid For It, I'm Gonna Eat It

Our group of Senior Saints climbed into the church van. We were tired and ready to go home after a five-day excursion to the Grand Canyon. I took my seat, but a moment later I squirmed around and tried to get comfortable. *I must have gained a pound a day on this trip.*

Why, oh, why had I eaten so much?

"I bit off more than I needed," I mumbled to my seat partner.

"Me, too. I think it's because we didn't have to cook. But wasn't that chocolate pie. . ."

"Enough. I don't want to hear another word about food. I overdid it the first day, and the second, and. . .well, it's time to call it quits."

I lost my willpower the first day. It had been a long drive and by the time we checked into our hotel we were hungry. Delicious smells met us at the cafeteria door and my mouth watered before I got to the hot food tables. One dish after another invited me to dig in. *Not too much*, I told myself, *there's more ahead*, so I took just a little—of each.

Roast beef in yummy brown gravy. Golden chicken. Pulled pork. I pushed the meat to the side of my plate and added a scoop of green beans and yellow corn. Jello, crisp lettuce with several dressings—none fat-free.

"Fruit, Ma'am?" a waitress asked. I smiled and stuck an apple in my pocket for later.

A smell like no other permeated the restaurant. I needed no one asking if I wanted a freshly baked roll.

Was there room for dessert? *Why not?* I added a small piece of chocolate cake. When I finally sat down with my over-laden plate, I wondered, *Why did I take so much? I'll take my time. Besides, I paid for it so I'm gonna eat it.*

Bit by bit, the food disappeared. I eyed my dessert dish. One forkful of the chocolate cake, another and still another, until finally, I washed the last piece down with a mouthful of coffee. I stared at my empty plate while my stomach told me I had bitten off more than I should chew.

I should have learned my lesson. Four more meals were on the schedule. Plus cheese, crackers and fruit on the train ride to the canyon as well as the return trip to the hotel. Whatever was offered, I ate. After all, I had paid for it.

On the van ride home, I paid again—for over-indulgence. . .

Too late, I discovered there is a way to conquer this greed. One particular slice of God's fruit of the Spirit will do it: Self-control, Galatians 5:22-23.

Prayer

Heavenly Father, getting my money's worth often ends up by losing my self-control. Forgive me for being greedy, Father, and help me choose Your way, the best way. Amen.

A Step Further

For the kingdom of God is not a matter of eating and drinking, but of righteousness, peace and joy in the Holy Spirit.
Romans 14:17 (NIV)

Moving On

The dinner table beckons me.
So does God's kingdom.

Question

What puts the biggest smile on my face, getting my money's worth, or getting what is free, God's abundant life?

WISDOM, GRACE AND WRINKLES

Laugh in the Face of Life

Aging? For or Against?

The older I get, the more confusing life gets. Computers agitate me the most. Cell phones, iPads (don't have one, thank you), even the remote control for the TV drive me battier than I already am. I managed to find Netflix once (once was enough), when my daughter went to see her grandkids. I chose a movie, watched it to the end, then punched a button. . .then another, then still another. After an hour of hitting one button after another, I landed back on regular TV. I wiped away the perspiration, turned the TV off, and went to bed to dream of monsters with TVs for heads.

It's not just confusion. There's fear. I'm afraid my daughter is going to say, "Hand 'em over. Your driver's license and your car keys. Now." Poof. There would go my independence. Hasn't happened yet, but I'm getting almost too careful when driving. Probably giving the driver behind me road rage.

Aging. What a nasty word! It conjures up visions—wrong word. Visions are lovely—vision weakens. Aging focuses on thinning hair. And on brown spots. Change that to white spots between brown discolorations. And did you know clothes shrink when they hang in the closet? They no longer fit in the right places. Under protest, my clodhopper shoes and a cane are often necessary. My weepy eyes force me to convince the people I meet, "No. Honest. I'm not sad."

Oh, and how about forgetfulness? Used to be I could laugh and say, "Oops. A senior moment." Now, when I haul the breakfast cereal out of the refrigerator, I do it when no one is looking. And before I start looking for my misplaced glasses I touch my eyes—just in case I'm wearing them.

This thing called aging is the final chapter of my life. Confusion, being overly cautious, my deteriorating body and forgetfulness bug me, until I remember these are momentary. My walk may be jerky, my eyesight may be growing dim, but up ahead I see a bright light. It is leading me to eternity.

That's when I start to giggle. Yeah, you got it . . . giggle. I have an excuse for all my mishaps these days. A viable, excusable reason to get away with just about anything. I find laughing easier as I age. Call it life experience. I've already been through it all, seen the poo life can toss, but more so, I can see the humor in my mistakes now. Laughing for me at this stage in life is a taunt, a ha-ha, been there done it, own the tee-shirt, place.

It's not something you see coming in midlife. Age just sorta sneaks up on you. And at times it angers me I can't do the things I once did, but so what? It's my time to be. . .pampered a bit. I suppose age is God's way of beefing me up for eternity.

Wow. Foggy thinking, wishing I looked younger, forgetfulness, all wiped away by God and replaced by clear thinking, laughter at my silliness and filling my mind with newness.

When I think about my husband and several of my friends who are already in heaven, I wonder what they are up to. Standing before the throne and praising Jesus? Relaxing? Doing what they did on earth and improving minute by minute? A giggle builds up in me. Laughter spills from my mouth. Up ahead, not too far down the road, I'm going to exchange this old me for someone new where aging is a "No" word. Best of all, there I'll meet Jesus, my Creator and Savior, face to face. Imagine that!

Do not cast me off in the time of old age; do not forsake me when my strength fails.

Psalm 71:9 (NASB)

Whose Glove is This?

Sometimes when I say, "Ah, to be young again," memories nudge me. How could I have forgotten the hectic days of raising three sons and a daughter? A poem I once read seemed to be written especially for me:

"I'm wearing a glove that does not fit my hand."

I'm still wearing that glove. Today I looked in the mirror and wished I hadn't. My wrinkled face, the brown liver spots on my hands, the squinty look in my eyes, made me want to run and hide. *How can this be? This glove belongs to someone else.* I rubbed the sagging skin on my cheek.

"David, I'm getting old," I said to my grandson.

"Gran'ma," he said, "no offense, but you and your youth haven't been on the best of terms lately."

My grandson—the joy (?) of my life—hit me with his *no hiding, no denying* attitude.

His words and my visit to an assisted living home further opened my eyes.

Each week, several ladies in the assisted living complex come to listen as I play hymns on my tape player. Susan, one of the elderly women, propelled her wheelchair into the room, a little late. She ran her hand through her thinning strands of hair.

"I used to have curly hair," she said. "Now, I can't do anything with it."

A friend reached down and squeezed her shoulder. "And that's our biggest concern today?" she said.

Susan glanced down at her feet. She strained to lift the feet that she could no longer control. Her sigh touched my heart. "If that were all," she said.

Her friend's question traveled home with me. What was my biggest concern? Wrinkles, brown spots, squinty eyes? Who cares? Well, me a little, but don't tell.

My health is good, though I could stand a little sympathy when my back hurts or my leg cramps when I stretch. And. . .oh, never mind.

I checked the mirror for another look. This time I laughed. These aging bodies will change when Jesus comes again. Aches and pains will disappear. I can put up with them for the moment, but my pity-party made me forget something important.

Something God said. *". . .for God sees not as man sees, for man looks at the outward appearance, but the Lord looks at the heart."* I Samuel 16:7 (NASB)

Prayer

Father God, help us know it doesn't matter how old we look on the outside if our hearts are clean inside, because You will never stop loving us. Thank You, God. Amen.

Moving On

…. but I will not forget you. Behold, I have inscribed you on the palms of my hands.
Isaiah 49:15b, 16a (NAS)

Question

Do you dare look in the mirror and smile?
Remember, God's mirror is better.

Discretion is a life-giving fountain to those who possess it, but discipline is wasted on fools.

Proverbs 16:22 (NLT)

Do I Hafta Do It?

My great-granddaughter, Julia, hated the idea of going to a new school. It meant entering fourth grade without her regular friends. "Do I hafta go?" she asked her mother.

Her mother hugged her. "Yes, of course," she said. "Don't worry. You'll find new friends."

Julia sighed. "I'll take a book along to read when it's lunchtime. Then even if I sit alone I can read."

Two days later, Julia found a friend and the scary start to a new school, new classmates and a new teacher faded away.

I vaguely recall being in the fourth grade. I, too, was shy and afraid, but I learned the things I had to do usually turned out okay.

Aging sneaked up on me, and still there are things I hafta do. Like Julia, many of these make me want to say, "Do I hafta do this?"

No ifs, ands, or buts. I hafta do it.

1. Take vitamins to stay strong and prescription pills to keep me healthy. *A chocolate reward helps the medicine go down.*

2. Follow doctor's orders: Walk. *Does parking your car at least three minutes from the grocery store door count?* Exercise at the pool. *It's called Twinges in the Hinges.* Get a yearly check-up. *Make sure my doctor listens as I whine.*

3. See the eye doctor; have possible cataract surgery. *As the wolf said to Little Red Riding Hood, "The better to see you with, my dear."*

4. Obey my kids. *A really difficult one:* "Don't get on that step-stool." "Do not vacuum." "I don't want you driving to Denver." *I didn't want to clean those cupboards or vacuum anyway. And the Highway Department must have stretched the highway these last few years.*

5. Erase pride and accept a helping arm or use a cane so I don't fall. *So says Proverbs 16:18. Pride goes before destruction and a haughty spirit before a fall. . .(NIV)*

6. Now comes the hardest admonition of all: the Lord says, "Be holy as I am holy." *This one, however, is not a "Do I hafta?" but an* "I really want to."

Prayer

Father, those first five rules are for my physical health. The sixth one is for my spiritual health. With Your Holy Spirit's help, I will obey. Amen.

A Step Forward

Let your eyes look directly forward, and your gaze be straight before you.
Proverbs 4:25 (RSV)

Moving On

Replace "hafta" with "will do."

Question

Am I letting aging get the better of me?

There is a time for everything, a season for every activity under heaven.

Ecclesiastes 3:1 (NLT)

Surprise!

The month of August carried an abundance of green beans in her arms. Each one needed to be washed, steamed, and frozen. Together, my daughter and I filled containers and put them in the freezer for next winter.

Next, red, juicy tomatoes came to life. Ummm, the taste of those lettuce, bacon and tomato sandwiches lingers in my mind while the salsa my daughter cooked up adds spice to our meals.

Soon after, peaches ripened and my daughter headed to the orchards. I love frozen peaches, and freezing them became my job.

After standing for half an hour, peeling and cutting the peaches into quarters, I wondered, why had I suggested this? My back ached. I shifted from my left side to my right. And back again. I stretched and stared at the rest of the peaches with disgust. That's when surprise hit me.

I'd been denying it, but old age had crept into my life. I glanced once more at the remaining fruit. "Tomorrow is another day. They won't spoil overnight." I put my paring knife in the sink, washed my hands and headed for my recliner to lose myself in a good book.

The next day, my daughter was off from work. I sat at the kitchen table and watched as the peaches jumped from her hands into the freezer boxes.

Did I feel guilty letting Jo Anne do all the work? Maybe a bit. But as Solomon says in Ecclesiastes 3:1, there is a time for everything.

Words from an old song popped into my head—"The old gray mare ain't what she used to be."

How true. As Solomon said, there *is* a time for everything. Now is the time to watch and smile and think how nice, as someone younger and more able does what I no longer need to do. I'm no longer surprised by age. If this is what getting older brings, I'm all for it. Let's relax and let go.

Prayer

Giver of all gifts, the ones of youth and the ones of age, thank you for allowing me to do all I did for my family. Thank you, too, for those who are now taking my place. Amen.

A Step Further

He will take these weak mortal bodies of ours and change them into glorious bodies like His own, using the same mighty power that He will use to conquer everything, everywhere.
Philippians 3:21 (NLT)

Moving On

Enjoy what you accomplished. Enjoy what others are doing.

Question

Do I let aging smother my laughter?

But let all who take refuge in You be glad, let them ever sing for joy; and may You shelter them, that those who love Your name may exult in You.

Psalm 5:11 (NASB)

Be Happy

Seventy-five years ago, a heart-stirring radio program about Jesus touched me. In an instant, I turned into a wanna-be missionary.

It was out of the question. I was only fourteen. I would have to wait until I finished high school and college.

"Poppa," I said. "I have to do *something* for God. But I'm too young to do anything special." Tears dripped down my cheeks.

Dad smiled and hugged me. "Ah, Betty, you're not too young to do one special thing. Maybe that's all God will ever ask of you."

"What?" I asked. "What would that be?"

He smiled and gave me a simple answer. "Just do whatever He tells you. Perhaps all God will ever ask of you is to be happy."

Be happy? All the time. Was it possible? When my brother teased me about some boy, or my mother made me take my younger sister along when I wanted to meet my friends, I shoved happiness to the side and wore a frown instead.

I wished I could be like my dad. I heard his happy whistle when he went to work and when he returned home at 5:30. Every summer he traveled the state of Michigan, selling perennials to nurseries. Sometimes I rode with him and waited in the car with a book until he emerged from the office where he was presenting the product. Did he make a sale? His whistle said yes. If his whistle was missing, I'd know the plants hadn't found a home. No matter. When he saw me waiting, he would smile and whistle again.

My dad did what he told me to do. He let God direct his ways and was happy.

As I look back I see a girl, then a woman, now an old lady and with a grateful heart. I see I have been—and am—happy. Sure, ruts and bumps in the road sometimes slowed me or forced me to change direction. Heartpains caused me to say, "Father, I'm losing it. Help me." I turned to Him and God sent my smile back.

God never did ask hard things of me. He gave me joy and I accepted it. It has been an umbrella over the good and sad times in my life. If, by being happy I have served God, then I am indeed, truly joyful.

Maybe we can't whistle, but if we open our hearts, we'll let the joy of the Lord flow in and overflow into the lives of others.

Prayer

God, You have passed this gift of happiness to me through my dad and I am grateful. Help me share it with others. In Jesus' name I pray, Amen.

A Step Further

I have God's more-than-enough ...
Psalm 4:7a (The Message)

Moving On

Smile. You're on God's camera.

Question

Does my happiness show?

... those who hope in the Lord will renew their strength. They will soar on wings like eagles; they will run and not grow weary, they will walk and not grow faint.

Isaiah 40:31 (NIV)

Sometimes You May Say No

This morning I turned off the alarm, pulled the blankets around me, then dozed back into dreams. Thirty minutes later, I jolted from my sleep. "Bible study class begins in one hour." I showered in "not quite" hot water, dressed and ate a skimpy breakfast. Never mind making the bed. Do it later.

I grabbed my Bible lesson off the end table, thankful I had finished it yesterday. Ten minutes to nine. Well, better late than never. Then it hit me. *It's the first of the month and most of the bills are due in a few days. I needed stamps.*

My head hurt, and I plopped down in the nearest chair. There was too much going on. I was overbooked, and it was nobody's fault but mine. I was the one who said, "Yes, I'll do a program at the assisted living home each week."

The Bible study class? No one forced me to sign up for it.

As for the swim therapy class, the doctor's firm voice echoed in my ears. "I want a checklist from the person in charge so we can see how you are doing."

But the Mission Board meeting, the Sunday school study, the cooking, cleaning, letters and calls to friends—I couldn't. I just couldn't do it all.

Relax. Do what you should have done in the first place—ask God for wisdom and direction.

Did I trust Him? Absolutely. A prayer rose from my heart, "Heavenly Father, I need Your help."

My anxious thoughts disappeared, and I accomplished what needed to be done. Hereafter I determined to ask God for direction before the day got started. Since I had already committed myself to certain things, I would rely on God to give me strength to finish what I had started.

As to the future, I am not irreplaceable. The time has come to say, "Sorry. I can't help right now."

We can save ourselves much unnecessary concern if we come to God before we find ourselves in trouble. He is the God of the possible.

Prayer

Heavenly Father, how glad I am I can depend on You. I need not try to do everything. From now on help me choose what it is You want me to do. In Jesus' name, I pray. Amen.

A Step Further

Commit to the Lord whatever you do,
and your plans will succeed.
Proverbs 16:3 (NIV)

Moving On

Let His plans shed light on mine.

Question

Do I plunge ahead or do I acknowledge His leadership?

Now we see but a poor reflection as in a mirror; then we shall see face to face. Now I know in part; then I shall know fully, even as I am fully known.

I Corinthians 13:12 (NIV)

Mirrors

The mirrors in my house have to go. Lately, nasty beings have sneaked into my home, removed my mirrors and replaced them with the fun house kind. They may make you laugh for a moment, but they also twist and distort the faces of those who look into them.

I have proof. Each time I see myself in the bathroom mirror or the gold framed one in the hallway, I glance over my shoulder. *Where did the real me go?* The spotted, wrinkled, aged face reflected in the mirror can't possibly belong to the clear-skinned, smooth-faced young woman my husband married.

Yup. The mirrors have to go. What I can't see won't hurt me. Do you suppose what should trouble me more than mirrors is something I cannot discard or hide? It's what God sees when He looks at me.

When Samuel looked for a kingly man to replace Saul, God told him, "Man looks at the outward appearance, but the Lord looks at the heart." I may try to hide from my physical appearance, but I cannot hide my wrong desires, my nasty thoughts about others, my "white" lies from God.

What He wants to see is a heart like the one Jesus has. He wants me to be holy as He is holy. Impossible? Not if I use the Bible. There I'll see Jesus. If I follow Him through the gospels, my walk will, in time, mirror His walk. My life will reflect His loving kindness to others.

May God see the kind of heart He is looking for.

Prayer

Father, I am Your child now. I cling to Your promise that someday I will be like Jesus, the kind of person You want me to be. I can hardly wait. In His precious name, Amen.

A Step Further

And just as we have borne the image of the earthly man, so shall we bear the image of the heavenly man.
1 Corinthians 15:49 (NIV)

Moving On

Change may take a lifetime.

Question

Does the mirror of my heart reflect Jesus?

The Lord Himself goes before you and will be with you; He will never leave you nor forsake you. Do not be afraid; do not be discouraged.

Deuteronomy 31:8 (NIV)

Loneliness

Chatter from the neighborhood get-together filled the air. Anne and Rob had invited me to the pot-luck, along with some of their other friends. A dozen people gathered in twos and threes. They were seated on benches, on folding chairs, or standing together. Everyone talked, hugged, and laughed. Everyone but me.

The sounds swirled around me and a feeble smile grew on my face. Anne headed for the kitchen just as I entered the yard. Her husband fried hamburgers on his grill with two of his buddies who told him the right way to do it. People I knew best, my next-door neighbors, were gone for the weekend and the others were casual acquaintances, the kind you waved at whenever you drove by. No one in the group approached me. No one said, "Hello."

I stuffed my hands in my pockets. Took them out again. Nobody noticed me. Soon all the talk became like tennis balls, batted back and forth, back and forth, while I stood in the center—alone—an invisible net over which the balls flew.

A chilly breeze touched my back and I wished I had worn my sweater, wished I had stayed home.

Loneliness came over me. Disturbing thoughts spun through my head. *Where do I belong? Not here. I don't know these people. They don't know me. I have no idea what they are talking about. Why did I come?*

I turned to leave just as Anne came to the rescue. "Betty. Why are you just standing there? Come over and meet some of the others." With her words and her arm in mine, loneliness drifted out of the gathering.

Am I the only one with these feelings? It even happens to royalty. Queen Wilhelmina of the Netherlands wrote a book entitled *Lonely, But Not Alone.* She, a royal personage, often felt lonely. In her book, she explained why she could add, *not alone* to book's title: she knew God was with her.

It applies to us as well. In the book, *The Name of the Promise is Jesus*, Michael Card writes, "Every time we let loneliness take over our feelings, we have lost sight of that personal, caring, and loving Father."

Remember: God is anywhere we are. Always. He will not forsake us.

Prayer

Heavenly Father, thank You for taking away my loneliness. When my mind stays on You I do not feel alone. In Jesus' name I pray. Amen.

A Step Further

Blessed be the Lord, Who bears our burdens and carries us day by day, even the God
Who is our salvation.
Psalm 68:19 (Amplified)

Moving On

God is always beside us.

Question

To whom do I turn when I am lonely?

Now, When It's All Said and Done

I hope you'll take time to enjoy life while you have the opportunity. Remember the wisdom of one who has walked the road ahead of you, stumbled over the same rocks, and scraped her knees until blood trickled down her leg.

Keep these little tid-bits close to your heart.
* Rise each morning only to fall to your knees in prayer
* Forgiveness is a must
* Tell those close to you how much you love them
* Choose your battles—some are just not worth the effort
* But most importantly. . .

        Dare to Laugh.

Elizabeth

Elizabeth Van Liere's articles, stories and poems have been published in various magazines for over sixty years. At age 87, her first book, *Dare to Live*, was published. Written for those "over the hill, but not under it," the book dwells on the frustrations for those on the other side of 60. Because Elizabeth believes God has given her a gift of laughter, she shares insights in this latest book, *Dare to Laugh – Devotions for those Full of Year*. From the small, nagging irritations to tears-in-your-heart trials, she turns the focus on problems to God's plan for our lives. At age 91 she passes on a glimpse of why we *Dare to Laugh*.